PRAISE FOR *DISPATCH FROM THE FUTURE*

"I love these poems. They are cool and horrified at their own coolness. A masterclass in phrase-making." —JOE DUNTHORNE, FABER NEW POET AND AUTHOR OF *SUBMARINE*

"Leigh Stein's poems know how to laugh it off after a stunning tumble down a flight of stairs." —ROB MACDONALD, EDITOR OF *SIXTH FINCH*

"*Dispatch from the Future* is a force of nature. Like other great American poets before her—Bernadette Mayer, Jorie Graham, William Carlos Williams come to mind—Leigh Stein is not afraid to make the everyday beautiful. As if she says in these poems, 'Don't worry, we all feel this way.' We do. Read this book." —DOROTHEA LASKY, AUTHOR OF *AWE* AND *BLACK LIFE*

PRAISE FOR LEIGH STEIN'S *THE FALLBACK PLAN*

"Beautiful, funny, thrilling and true." —GARY SHTEYNGART, AUTHOR OF *SUPER SAD TRUE LOVE STORY*

"*The Fallback Plan* is to this generation what Rick Moody's *The Ice Storm* was to the previous generation, and *The Catcher in the Rye* before that." —SUSAN SALTER REYNOLDS, *LOS ANGELES REVIEW OF BOOKS*

"Stein, 26, captures the voice of the young 20-something prodigal daughter with the clarion call of authenticity in her debut novel. . . . Stein's light, accessible, self-deprecating prose makes this coming-of-age story a pleasure." —*PUBLISHERS WEEKLY*

"Cheeky self-assured prose." —*O: THE OPRAH MAGAZINE*

"A masterwork of the post-collegiate babysitting genre."
—*NEW YORK MAGAZINE*

"Her enchantingly funny and insightful debut novel *The Fallback Plan* ... has a universal quality, capturing a generation's angst quite like *Franny and Zooey* did when it was published in 1961."
—*CHICAGO TRIBUNE*

"27-year-old former *New Yorker* staffer Leigh Stein nails the latest postcollegiate trend—moving back in with Mom and Dad... Stein seems poised to become the Lena Dunham of contemporary fiction, given the way *The Fallback Plan*'s storyline deftly bears with it a steady commentary on today's flatlining economy and a generation of college grads (an estimated 85 percent of the class of 2011 moved right back home) who have to wonder if we'll ever actually grow up and become real adults."
—*ELLE MAGAZINE*

"Readers will endorse Esther Kohler's voice as being not only funny, but also true. It echoes long after her story ends, and *The Fallback Plan* is a novel everyone under 30 will relate to with familiar pangs of self-loathing and sympathy."
—*BOSTON GLOBE*

"Intimate, urgent, and laugh-out-loud funny, Leigh Stein's novel bravely investigates the splendor and tragedy of the end of youth with a sensitivity and lyrical deftness that will not disappoint. Think *Franny and Zooey*. Think *Goodbye, Columbus*. Think of this book as your next great read."
—JOE MENO,
AUTHOR OF *THE GREAT PERHAPS*

"...an existential crisis of lost 20-somethings that pretty much everyone can relate to."
—*NYLON MAGAZINE*

DISPATCH FROM THE FUTURE

For Andrew –
The future is
coming!!!

DISPATCH

FROM THE

FUTURE

POEMS BY LEIGH STEIN

MELVILLE HOUSE
BROOKLYN, NEW YORK

DISPATCH FROM THE FUTURE

First Melville House printing: June 2012

Melville House Publishing
145 Plymouth Street
Brooklyn, NY 11201

www.mhpbooks.com

ISBN: 978-1-61219-134-8

Manufactured in the United States of America

1 2 3 4 5 6 7 8 9 10

Library of Congress Cataloging-in-Publication Data

Stein, Leigh, 1984-
Dispatch from the future / Leigh Stein.
   p. cm.
ISBN 978-1-61219-134-8
I. Title.
PS3619.T465D57 2012
811'.6--dc23
                    2012014733

For Sarah

TABLE OF CONTENTS

I

IV

I

If you attempt to back out of the planet, turn to page 77.

If you decide to take the time to consider other options, turn to page 50.

If you attempt to back out of the planet, turn to page 77.

If you decide to take the time to consider other options,
turn to page 50.

Edward Packard, *Through the Black Hole*

WARNING

There are better ways to break a heart than Facebook,
such as abandoning your pregnant girlfriend at Walmart
like that guy did to Natalie Portman. If you read this book
sequentially, bad things may happen to you, but only as bad
as the things that would have happened to you anyway.
If, however, you do not read this book sequentially you may
find that you are suddenly aboard a sunken pirate ship,
staring into the deep abyss, and wishing you had chosen
not to chase the manatee in your submarine after all. Do not
panic. If you end up in the wrong adventure just go back
three spaces and draw another card. Or go back to bed.
Or read up on the side effects of the medication taken
by your loved ones. The great R. A. Montgomery once wrote,
"Suddenly you're surrounded by eleven Nodoors," and I
guess what I'm trying to do here is ruin any hope
you may have had of coming out of this alive.

BASED ON A BOOK OF THE SAME TITLE

By definition of vicious infinite regression
I don't like to talk to philosophy majors.
They have found the truth and the truth is

that there isn't one, so on Saturdays they
wear overalls and stare at their reflections
and try to guess whose childhood was worse,

but in the end they realize they all share
the same dream of having a reason
to join the Witness Protection Program,

which disappoints at least one person, who
thought his dream was so uniquely his.
Last night I got a fortune cookie that said

I don't get along with basically anyone,
and from the back I learned the Chinese word
for grape: *putao*, and it made me wonder how each

informs the other. To find out, turn to page 117.
I wonder how much longer I can live here
before I do something irresponsible like

meet a teenage boy on a Ferris wheel in 1941
or lie in the street and watch the stoplights
change from green to yellow or sit on a porch

swing at dusk and listen to *Leaves of Grass*
read by someone who has just worked all day
with his hands. Already on page 56 I love you

so much I just want to steal your clothes
when you're asleep and wash them. I want us
to communicate telepathically until I am old

and suffering from dementia and can't even
remember I know how to play piano until
a nurse tells me I do and still I'll deny it

until she puts my hands on the keys and then
there'll be Chopin so quickly, as the light
spills in the leaded windows and the lilies

lean in closer. By definition of vicious
infinite regression I am in front of a mirror
holding a copy of the movie based on the book

you wrote based on the parts of our life
together that I no longer remember and
looking back at me is a woman holding

a movie based on a book based on her life
and she wonders if the woman she sees
wants to die as much as she does. I keep

staring at this bruise on my leg and drawing
a blank. Last night when you called I told you
I was happy, which was true, but thinking ahead

I could be unhappy, too, if that's what you
wanted. I could be any of a lot of things:
a wrist, a ghost, a harbor, a rope. I could

be the one who doesn't know the language.
I could be the reason they take you first.
I could be the last person to see you alive.

Theoretically, I was held by a man in Detroit
at gunpoint. Theoretically, he let me go.

I have not told this story to you before.

I only tell you now for two reasons. One:
you're not from Michigan. Two: I have searched

for his scar along your neck and, so far, no luck.

They said to wear my purse beneath my coat and
pretend it was a baby if anybody asked me and

they might but they probably would not try and take it.

They said the average memory span for normal adults
is seven items. Let me differentiate between the two.

I used to tell this story about Tristan and Dolores,

who I left in the rain every time. I made them break blue
glass with their back teeth. Dolores would say, I am half sick

of shadows, as the waves came up from the storm tossed sea.

Try telling this story to a man with a gun. Sorry to interrupt,
he said, but do you know the one about the woman who

was rolled up like a snowman and left until the thaw?

No, I said. That was me, he said. I don't believe you, I said,
and then he told me to keep my hands above my head.

The snow had begun to fall then in the deep stillness

before the streets were plowed and salted; a car passed
us and fishtailed ahead at the stoplight; I forgot

the ending, and so I pushed my characters in front of a train.

The man with the gun didn't like that at all.
How was there a train at the beach? Maybe they left

the beach, I said. Should they go on vacation instead?

The man said, What if they went in front of the train, but
the train stopped in time. Good idea, I said. He read

my name off my drivers license and I didn't correct

his pronunciation; then he told me to close my eyes and
I felt something cold hit my head. My heart stopped a little

bit. When I opened my eyes, he was gone. There was

a snowball at my feet. Where did you say you were from again?
I just wanted to unbutton your collar and see for myself.

This time last year I was an astronaut
in a window display at a department store
that has since been bought out by another
department store. I wore a gray crepe dress
and a helmet that they pumped full of oxygen.
I had one line to say. I mouthed the words, but
no one ever heard me. They tapped the glass,
saying, We can't hear you on this side. Take
off the helmet. Take off my helmet? I mouthed
back. What?, they said. This time last year I
thought I was speaking English, but lip reading
has become a forgotten art. This time last year
I learned to speak in the dark with my hands.
I know the sign for tree and forest; dead bird;
the spelling of my maiden name; long walks
on the beach of Normandy. You think everything's
about you and you've been right since the end
of the war. I took that astronaut job so I could
tell you I took it. I took that astronaut job so I
could miss you from the cosmos beyond the glass.
This time last year it was snowing when you kneeled
to lace my skates and it was so nice to run into each other
under our pseudonyms like that. I said, Times of duress
call for a record. You said, Did you say something? No,
I said. You said, Why don't you take off that helmet?

I can't hear you when you do that thing with your mouth.
What thing with my mouth?, I said, and you closed your
eyes. And you held both my hands so if I tried to spell
our names you wouldn't see. I cut the number of my age
in ice. Will I ever be any older? No. I will not. Where
you're from they're cosmonauts, but you're the one
who left, I said. I could feel the oxygen running low.
The snow blanketed the totality of all existing things.

ZELDA

I want Rattawut Lapcharoensap to write my biography.
I want him to come to my apartment when my boyfriend's

not home. I want to make him coffee. I know that he
will want to tape record all of our sessions, and

after I die I want these tapes catalogued and archived
in the temperature controlled basement of an ivy league

university library. Additionally, I would like
my biography to have a neon purple dust jacket and

I would like Nancy Milford to grant us permission
to call the book *Zelda* even though there is already

a book called *Zelda* because it is about the life of Zelda
Fitzgerald. Maybe because it is just one word and

that word is a name we won't need permission; I'm
not a lawyer. Also: I would like Martin Scorsese to direct

the movie based on the book based on my real life.
I don't know if any of you have seen *The Departed* yet, but

I just saw it last night and my life is almost exactly like that
except instead of Boston I grew up in Chicago, and instead

of going to police academy I toured with Cirque du Soleil.
If Rattawut could just get a hold of a copy of the screenplay

and make Matt Damon a female trapeze artist
who was born to Prussian immigrant parents in 1984,

I'm sure he'd have a good three, four chapters right there, easy.
Have any of you ever tried to think of all the different ways

you could disappoint your parents and then done them?
I chose the calliope over the violin; I ran with gypsies;

I dated a boy three years younger than me just because
he had an apartment and I didn't want to live

with my parents anymore. I want Rattawut to tell me
he likes my blue sweater. Maybe I'll sit next to him

while I show him old photographs and wait to see
if he puts his hand on my leg. I don't know what will happen

to me after I turn 23, but when my biography comes out
I will have to avoid the reviews and the interviews

and any website that gives away the ending.
I will probably have to spend a few weeks in a cabin

in Minnesota. By then, I will have broken up
with my boyfriend in order to marry Rattawut

beneath a chuppah in the western suburbs of Chicago
because even though I'm not technically Jewish,

my father is, and any tradition is better than none.
When Rattawut gives me my autographed copy,

I'll stay inside my childhood, making daisy chains,
enrolled in summer programs for the gifted and talented.

I'll concentrate on the photos of myself holding prize ribbons,
playing leapfrog, dressed up like Elizabeth Cady Stanton.

I won't read the chapters about my future addiction
to pain medication, my lepidopterophobia,

my failed marriages, my miscarriages, the fire
that will destroy all my manuscripts, my fall

down the stairs. I won't ever read the last chapter,
the one that describes in vivid detail the flames

that will erupt from my fatal motorcycle accident
somewhere in the Badlands, how it will take weeks

for them to discover my body. I am only 22 years old.
I want to fake my death on Facebook. I want a pony.

Excellent customer service means never crying
in front of the customer, asking him to call or

send orchids. In a photograph taken during the time
when you knew all the constellations, you look

like you knew it would end up like this—stars
are something to talk about at night on a beach.

When they tell you they're from Nepal you say
you love Nepal. You love Flint, Michigan, you

love that there are roads and wrists and reasons
for the planets and no matter what they tie you to,

if afterwards you run into one on the bus, because maybe
you live in the same neighborhood, you will hold

your suitcase handle because first of all, you
could be any of five names and second of all,

your accordion is in the suitcase and you have a ticket
to Valencia. Tomorrow you will be where the cliffs jut

from the sea. You've been practicing. If the stranger
sits beside you and says, Bangladesh, don't show

that you remember, get off before your stop, before
he says he has a fencepost, a red parachute, an open field.

EVEN THE GAS STATION ATTENDANT HERE IS NICE TO ME

I lost my job at the factory, but before you get mad
I want you to know that last night I woke up in the snow
without shoes, and I didn't call up to your window;
I let you sleep because I remembered our agreement.

This is what happened: he caught me in the freezer
with his copy of *Ulysses* and asked me what I thought
I was doing. What could I be doing, I said, what
are my options. I still had on my latex gloves

and I know you won't want to hear this part, but
I opened a carton of macaroons with my teeth.
You have always wanted to do that, he said. Yes,
I said. He said, I can't let you do that. So I ate one.

He turned off the lights. I took a yellow cake
off a shelf and lit twenty candles to warm our hands.
How is this night different from all other nights?
There was a time when I didn't have to sleepwalk

everywhere. You remember. I was here. But
then I got used to waking up every morning
in a different city, without you, without the same
sun, the same lack of a view, all that scaffolding,

none of the sea, every piece of mail a sympathy card.
I can never go back there. I stole his book. When you
go to work each morning, I walk to Jerusalem.
I am answering your letter. You are ruining my life.

KATHARINE TILLMAN VS. LAKE MICHIGAN

Mitsu flips a lot of coins. Katharine told me that once
she was in the middle of a tantrum and a coin
told him he should love her, and yet, he wasn't
satisfied so he went to the dictionary and closed
his eyes and found a word and when she asked
what word he found, the only thing he would tell her
was that he was one step closer to the secret
of the universe. Can you tell me what it rhymes with,
she asked him. Is it a verb? Is it a country? Have I
been there? Will you write its name on my back
while we sit on the pier and watch the blue dusk
chase the sun to Jersey? The last time I ever
saw Katharine she asked me the name of the lake
in the distance and I said Michigan and she said
she'd heard of it, and then she showed me the diaries
she kept when she lived under the overpass
near Truth or Consequences, New Mexico,
when all she had was a travel Scrabble set and
the reason she'd run away. Milan Kundera
has a lot to say about our tenuous insignificance.
When he wants to decide something he, too,
flips a coin, but in his case heads is Little Rock,
Arkansas, and tails is Little Rock, Arkansas, and
it's just a matter of who to blindfold and bring with
on his motorcycle. On page one hundred and seven

of *The Unbearable Lightness of Being*, I get lost
driving Katharine to the airport. On page one hundred
and forty nine, Tereza dreams that they take her away.
After I see Katharine for the last time I don't go home;
I go to Prague and it's 1968 and the man I love won't
touch me; he just holds an empty gun to my temple
and even though we both know it's empty there's the small
comfort that the worst thing that could possibly happen
would be the thing I want most. Mitsu says the secret
of the universe is obvious in any planetary shaped
object you can find on the floor of a parking garage.
Katharine says how. I say I want to move to Canada;
the only tenderness anyone can get around here
is in the time it takes him to untie my wrists.

KEEPING THE MINOTAUR AT BAY

He takes me to a movie about a bathtub
full of Vaseline and apples and asks me

afterward how I feel about it. I feel pretty
ambivalent about the universe, I say,

like I've been reading too many wilderness
guides and spending all my nights

trapped in lucid dreams in which I'm
beneath the deepest, most inescapable

snowdrift and I decide to stay there until it melts
at the end of the world—*el fin del mundo,*

as they say, *acharit hayamim*—and the whole time
I'm dreaming I'm thinking, I can't wait

to get in my boat and sail across the flooded earth.
So, I tell him, I get in my canoe and all the old cities

are phosphorescent scars miles below the surface,
sunken ships without survivors, and I know

I won't last long. I know the end is near
and yet I paddle on, scanning the open seas

for a waterproof map, a yellow umbrella,
another survivor in another canoe, and I think this

is how disappointed everyone must have felt
when Atlantis sank. In the classic *Return to Atlantis,*

R. A. Montgomery writes, "Destruction is widespread,
and you grieve for the Atlantean people" (85). Don't I

know it. It's at this point in the dream when I realize I am
actually alone and likely to drown and I start to scream

and then I wake up in my own bathtub, water to my knees.
Another nightgown soaked. For the Norse, that's hell:

wearing a soaked nightgown in a cold, dark room
for eternity, I say, did you know that? He says

he didn't know, but that I seem like a very
interesting person for a person my age,

which makes me think Theseus must have
said something just like that to Ariadne,

to make her fall in love with him so she
would give him the red threaded clew

to the maze and he could slay the monster.
I used to think I was waiting for a steady shoulder,

for someone to come along and appreciate my
somnambulism, my prophetic knowledge

of the ultimate destiny of mankind, someone
to be with when all the lights in the world go out,

but look what happened to them. Theseus killed
the beast, and they got married and then sailed

to an island, where he abandoned Ariadne in her sleep.
And when she woke she hanged herself. Why

did she hang herself? And if I find the reason am I
less susceptible? Both unanswerable questions, and

yet I still go home with him, submit to a strange
bed in which I lay awake all night, without him,

listening to the restless pacing of something familiar
in the room beneath us, the haunt I cannot kill.

HOW TO MEND A BROKEN HEART WITH VENGEANCE

We stretched a ladder between our second-story
windows and tried to get the dog to go
across to see if it would hold but it didn't.

My ambivalence must have made the dog fall, I
called across to him. He picked up his tin can
and said, I can't hear you unless you speak

into the tin cans, remember? What did you just
say? *Sono spiacente*, I said. Nevermind. *Slicha.*
You are probably wondering now if the dog's okay,

but do you think you could stay with me, anyway,
even if I never gave you the answer? This was
so long ago, further back than yesterday,

when you and I spoke for the last time. You said,
Why did you leave so early? And I said I couldn't
sleep and you asked me why I didn't tell you

at the time; you would have hit me on the head
with something hard. Let me ask you, could you
imagine a cloudless sky above a Nebraska plain?

Could you draw it? Could you imagine yellow birds?
Could you visualize the soft sound a door
makes when it closes and sticks and I thought I

had problems, but seriously, look at yourself.
Look. I had this incredible dream last night
and I'm not even going to tell you about it.

In Russia, the young girls who die violent deaths
either end up like birds in Pushkin or like fish
at the bottom of lakes, where they comb each other's

hair all night long, where they teach each other
the lyrics to every Talking Heads song
so they can lure sailors into their shadowy grottoes

and drown them. They say there once was a rusalka
who wished to be human so badly she gave up
her voice to be with her beloved and of course

he loved her because who wouldn't love a girl
who can't talk back, but then one night
at a masked ball he got distracted by a foreign princess

with an elegant neck and the rusalka was so despondent
she went to a witch and somehow communicated, I've
never been so unhappy in my whole life. What should I do?

And of course the witch told her to stab him with a dagger,
and of course the rusalka considered it. Like, seriously?
Seriously stab him with a dagger? But ultimately she

decided she would rather lose her human life and
go back to being an underwater death demon.
At least in the opera version the prince realizes

his terrible mistake and goes hunting for a doe
only to find the rusalka in her last moments and
kisses her knowing it means death and eternal

damnation. Here I am now, watching the moonlight
dance across the water in the retention pond, staring
at this scalpel and trying to forget your address.

JUNE 14, 1848

Weather: hot. Health: fair.
Dear Diary, had to leave the baby
behind because she wouldn't eat.

Sent Jon out to shoot a buffalo,
but he said they all looked so peaceful
he couldn't bring himself to do it.

Figures. We'll all be dead soon
enough. Waiting for the Indian
to get here so we can cross

the river. June 15, 1848.
Weather: still hot. Health: same.
Dear Diary, Chastity's doll

drowned. She wanted to dive
in after it, but I reminded her
that she doesn't know how to swim.

Dove in anyway. Another one lost.
Jon says he'll skin us a buffalo
so we have something to eat, but

only if the buffalo has recently
died of natural causes. Get
a grip, Jon, I told him.

June 16: wagon broke.
Eating wild blackberries while
we wait for another wagon

party to come by and help.
Jon has gone off on his own
to meditate and ask forgiveness

of the earth. Prudence might
have dysentery. Figures.
June 17: Some days

I feel like I'm just a character
in a game played by a sick,
sick person, who has sent me

on this journey only to kill all
my loved ones along the way.
June 18: help came, but

in the night they stole our oxen.
Guess we'll just have to walk
to Oregon now. Are you there,

God? It's me, Mary Jane.
Send me some oxen and
a son who likes to shoot things.

June 19: Lost Prudence
to dysentery. Should we
eat her? Tough question.

June 20: Another river!
You have got to be kidding!
June 21: Managed to swim

across with diary on top
of my head so it wouldn't
get wet. Jon and I have found

a tribe of Indians who will let us
stay with them. At least,
we think that's what they said.

We don't speak their language.
They seem to have indicated that
tonight we must follow them,

blindfolded, into a grove of trees,
and in the addled darkness our
dead will return and speak to us.

Mother, I have been devastated all my life. I never said anything.
That's why I wear a parachute. Why I tiptoed from my bedroom
to yours, and lay my head on the beige carpet for fear of worse.
Were there sirens? There were. Were there familiar songs? Yes.
I am afraid of the beds I have been in. In the morning there was
the heel of your boot sharper than before. Mother, what do I do
with your mail? Do you want to keep this snake in the basement?
What about the kitten? Do you want all these photographs of other
people's children? The temperature in the lizard's cage is dropping.
Let's be realistic. If I open the windows the birds will come in and
eat out the eyes. Mother, I am bereft. Mother, I wear your necklace
and nothing else. Mother, I never. Nevermind. Let's be fatalistic.
The neighbors know I'm down here. I can hear them watching.
Mother, after they take your eyes I will sew the lids myself.

Count back by sevens beginning with the last number
you remember. I'll wait, said the Serbian Jew to the lame girl

who blushed at her wet shoes. West 72nd Street was a puddle
from Broadway to the Hudson and the traffic came and returned.

In Brooklyn you could lie in the street in front of the hospital
and not die. Sixty-three, she said, like a question of him.

For the last eleven hours I had worn a feathered headband
and taken dictation from a woman in Utah. I wanted

to know what had happened to the girl's leg, but I was also
thirsty. He had to know. If I were him I'd ask her every day.

The night the circus marches the elephants through midtown,
the girl would say, have you ever been? Yes, I would say,

once. Well, she would say. No. Yes. No. She might say
it wasn't an accident. Pretend to hold a knife in your hand

and people will think it's your own. Her cane was on my foot,
but I stood still. Fifty-six and forty-nine. If she had picked

a larger number to begin with, I could have stood with the cane on my foot forever. I was so cold then; I wore so many hats.

Can I get you something? His yarmulke was secured to his head with gold hairpins. No, I said. I don't know what I want, I said.

The girl stopped counting and apologized for her cane. Don't apologize, I said. Please, I said. It was a lion, she said. Forty-two,

I said, right? It was a land mine. I didn't ask, I said. It was my mother, she said, in our bathroom. Thirty-five? It was me. I did it. It was me.

Good news: you still won't leave your wife for me,
but there is a horse tethered to the scaffolding

in front of my building and I think he might be mine.

Stealing horses means never having to say I love you,
are you as awake as I am, will you pat my head or

something. Stealing horses means never having to ask

to be asked what you're thinking. Like now, for example,
when all I can think of is this neighborhood boy named

Morris, the one I can see from my window at night;

he asked me today what the horse's name was
and I said I'm afraid to name him in case he dies

and the boy said, It's like in those books with dogs

where you know something bad will happen and
I said, Exactly. He asked if we could go for a ride.

This is a stolen horse, I said, possibly from upstate.

I said I didn't know if it would be safe, but I
invited him up to my fire escape and we let our legs

hang off the edge and watched the ferryboats

in the harbor until dusk and the water darkened.
Have you always lived on this island?, I said,

pretending I didn't see he had a bruise on his arm,

and Morris said, I have a bruise on my arm, and I
said, Can I do anything?, and he said, When you're

at the museum are you ever afraid of falling

through the railings they have around the balconies?
I nodded. There is a cautionary tale about a woman

and a boy who comes to her birthday party to tell her

he is her husband who died in the park and by the time
she believes him he says nevermind. Morris, I said,

I think terrible thoughts about those that I love.

EURYDICE

i

In Philadelphia, a dying woman wants to know
a seven letter word for "don't look back."

Does it have to be in English?, her daughter
asks. Why, she says, what are you thinking?

I think it is seventy degrees in Alaska today.
Last night I went to a party to find a lawyer

to support me for the next thirty-seven years or so
or, if not a lawyer, at least someone to spend all these

relentless hours with me while I measure the rising
temperature of the sea. Do you want to know

what I do with these measurements?, I asked
one of my prospects. He didn't say he didn't, so

I told him I tear them into tiny pieces and make
papier-mâché masks of all my friends which end

up looking more like ducks or bears than people faces,
but at least I am doing my part in all this.

He said, I'm not actually a lawyer. I run a hotline
for people who live alone. You can call in the morning

and tell your dream to a machine. I can?, I said. Sure,
he said, and that's when I knew who to follow.

ii

This book I'm reading says I should set one small goal each day.
Yesterday I got out of bed like there was no tomorrow.

Today I may call you just to hear how you answer.
This book says I shouldn't have unrealistic expectations,

like the woman in the parable of the woman who was killed
by the serpent on her wedding day did. One day

she was running happily through a meadow and she thought
her whole life would be just like that, a handful of violets,

but as we know now anything that is too good to be true
is probably about to be bit by a serpent. Her husband

followed her to the underworld but couldn't bring her back,
didn't trust she'd follow. It was like she wanted to stay.

But I plan on leaving. I have been completing the last
of the crossword puzzles and taking a lot of hot baths.

I would love to come back as a faucet. Or a radiator or an ice
cube tray shaped like a dozen little fish. Everybody loves those.

But meanwhile I will follow you back from wherever
you find me. In the deepest valley. At the dreadful shore.

At the end of the world I want to be in Reykjavik together,
watching the long dark night break down our door.

II

Mutato nomine de te fabula narratur.

Horace

My favorite book is the one with the woman
who wears a balaclava every time she goes
under the viaduct because it's Canada, and
because she's married to a man who loves
her sister, and because if her family found her
under the viaduct, she would lose everything;
more than that, she would lose the end of the story
he began. *Il était une fois*, he said, there are rugs
made by children who go blind and turn
to crime, and/or rescuing sacrificial virgins
from the palace the night before the sacrifice.
Turn one page if you want to be the woman,
listening to the story, but you'll have to
keep the hat on. Turn three if you'd rather
be a girl alone in a bed, waiting. I was
always that girl: you're alone and
they've already cut out your tongue
and in the morning they'll take you
to the top of a high hill, so what can you
do but follow the blind boy, watch
as he puts the body of the strangled guard
in your bed, in your place, follow as he leads
you through the air ventilation system and over
the palace walls? I never chose any other way
because what could the woman do but love him

and listen to a story that wasn't about her.
After you get over the walls you run
through the darkness, the darkness that isn't
darkness to the blind boy because of his blindness,
the silent darkness to you who can't describe it,
you run until you turn the page, but then instead
of safety, a valley, the woman under the viaduct
puts her skirt on and goes back home and you think
you've ended up in the wrong story, but months later
she gets a phone call saying the man was killed
in the Spanish Civil War and that's the end
because the only person who knows
what happened to you is dead.

THE FORBIDDEN CHAMBER

There are things you do when left
alone you wouldn't otherwise do, like
leave the house without your phone or
marry someone you'll wish would leave you
later or throw a party like in the ancient legend
of the call girl who falls in love with a Fabergé egg
instead of her young employer. In this tale, she
steals it from the mantel of his Glencoe mansion
and carries it in her smooth, white hands
while she looks for hidden rooms to enter.
It is apparent how anyone could love her
forever if she didn't cost his parents so much
money. I'll be late for school, the guy says, please
be gone when I get home. There are things
you can do if you look like Rebecca De Mornay,
including do whatever you want, which means
stumbling upon a room she shouldn't ever see,
where the master of the house keeps an armoire
full of limbs of all the girls that came
before her and she drops the egg, which doesn't
shatter, but then the blood won't come off and
what is she supposed to do? He'll kill her, too.
No matter what she does he'll kill her, too,
and this is not only true of legends, but

also true of life: if you're pretty, if you go
where you're not supposed to, looking for things
not meant for your eyes, then you will have to explain
the blood on your hands somehow or else
have a few brothers to break down the door
when you are kneeling on an expensive rug
some day, and there is a famous movie star
standing above you with a great big knife.

EPISTOLAPHOBIA

Is one of the symptoms remembering the ghosts
one has seen? I am not going to sign my name
to this postcard because who knows whose eyes

will see it besides yours and you should know
who is in Mogadishu right now and who is not.
The passwords to my accounts are hidden

somewhere in the following true story.
When I was fourteen, my father promised
me to a man who lived in the forest.

I never went to his cabin; he always came
to mine. When he asked me why I never came
I said I did not know the way and so

he tied a rope to all the trees and asked my father
to see that I followed it. Sometimes we put ourselves
in danger just to live and tell about it.

And sometimes we put ourselves in danger
because our fathers betroth us to murderers.
When I finally found the house no one was home

so I hid and I waited. Blood as red as apples,
apples as red as blood, skin as white as snow,
snow as red as blood: no one has seen what I

have. My betrothed came home with some men
and a girl and I still have her finger to prove it.
(Is one of the symptoms a constant dull ache?

Don't answer that; I don't have an address.)
I ran out of his house when he fell asleep
and I kept her finger under my pillow and I did

not tell what I had seen. Sometimes we
are so close to running, but we do not;
we'd rather sleep on a piece of a body

than steal a boat in the middle of a moonless
night and sail to the northern country where
the people assume you've done no wrong,

but if you have done wrong, they forgive you,
always, and maybe one of them forgives you more
than the others, and he takes you on long walks

in shady arbors and you want to tell him how
much you like his sweater, but ever since
the forest you've been mute, so you write

how much you like his sweater with a stick
in the ground and he gives it to you
off his back. Then you start to write all

that's ever happened to you, but
the best parts disappear into the grass
and he doesn't give you anything else, but

he does say that maybe you should run away
and you think he means he will come with,
but when the stars are all out

and he's still not at the pier to meet you, you sail
from that barren land without him
and send letters to show you forgive him

for staying. Is one of the symptoms a feeling
like you've been here before? I have not
been to a place yet that was not somehow familiar.

This is the end. The sun is just coming up
over the sea. In the desert they dream of water
and snow-capped volcanoes. I dream of amnesia.

In the play everyone thought he was a Croat
because he said his girlfriend bled to death

in his arms, but when they re-enacted her death
it was a convenience store robbery. Can you imagine

being so disheartened? I can imagine bleeding to death
in someone's arms. You reminded me of my husband

just then, who has the same name as your friend.
Before we could marry, Raul traveled to Djibouti

and toiled in my father's salt fields for seven years.
For seven years we are on the sea but we are thirsty.

For seven years we ride our camels at dusk
across the desolation. How do I know you love me?

How do I know that when I sleep you don't write
letters to someone who can read them? Raul says

there is no wasteland he wouldn't cross barefoot
if I was crying on the other side: for seven years

we have no idea what's going on. How could we
have known, in the bliss of such tranquility,

the terrible awfulness which would befall us?
You tell me. At the end of seven years we marry

beneath a canopy of some breathtaking rocks; I
think of what a good story this will be for our children:

at the altar I said I love you and your father said,
How do I know? I said, the life expectancy here

is pretty low, Raul. My father told him not to
raise his voice at me and I removed my veil.

Let us dance, I said, until all the stars are out,
and we did, and that was the last night I saw him.

All I've ever wanted is to ask the same question.
To answer he sends me sealed, empty envelopes.

HOW TO READ THE SECRET LANGUAGE OF THE PHARAOHS

I am afraid that if they build a sarcophagus
exactly to your measurements and then

invite you to a party, the sarcophagus
will be there and you will climb inside

and fit and then they'll shut the lid
and throw you into the river and you

will drown and what will I do then?
I couldn't sleep alone after I saw the movie

about the chariots and bloody ostrich hunts,
in which one man kills his brother and the wife

of the dead one has to wander around the desert
until she has picked up every piece of his body

and put them back together with the magic
tricks she knows. He doesn't live, but

he does get to go to the underworld, and the rest
of the movie is all about her life as a priestess

because when she asked if she could go with
him he said no, but I know that if I put you

back together I would follow you
to the underworld even if you said

you didn't want me to, even if you said
there were not enough seats in your chariot

or riverboat or rickshaw because when two
people spend as much time together in a small,

enclosed space such as we have in this one,
they will follow each other to future small,

enclosed spaces. This is a pretty long book
inscription, but when you leave I want you

to keep this with you at all times, in case
you need a curse, a lament, a mirage

or incantation. To speak the name of the dead
is to make them live again. I will never forget

when I was just your sister in the acacia
tree of our childhood and at night the chariots

and thrones and arrows and birds and twins
in the stars foretold our future ruin. I've heard

it said that he who loves you swallows stones
for you while your enemy waits for you

to birth a son to avenge his father's death
by causing a tempest to flood the earth.

FOR THOSE WHO HAVE EVERYTHING, SAY IT WITH CONCRETE

I have been lost before, but not with this many broken bones,
and I had a brighter torch. If you were lying in wait in a cave
like I am, right now, in the darkness, and you didn't know

when the next sandstorm would be, and you didn't know
if the next morning the war would start, and you didn't
know how long your torch would last, would you still

write letters with your only hand that wasn't useless?
Yes. And let's say that at this point you still believe
that the person who has promised to come back

for you is coming. Let's say you haven't started
to wonder about your flare gun yet and what
it's good for inside the cave. Can anyone ever

foresee that they will end up like this, in love
with a faceless, amnesiac cartographer?
I have learned from the Sahara the necessity

of white dresses and small airplanes. They didn't
think I belonged, but I waited my whole life to see
the ancient drawings of the ancient people swimming

in the ancient place. I was not in Italy, swinging
from a chapel ceiling. I was not in Cairo, bathing
in a clawfoot tub, because that hadn't happened

yet. I was just in love with the one person I wasn't allowed:
you, who I write letters to while I hemorrhage to death
in a place that no one knows exists. It is not on any map.

The map has not been made. I am starting to think that
the only way I'll ever be found is if you, the cartographer,
trade your topographical secrets, your photographs, your

name, to the Nazis in exchange for a jeep. Please. The light
is fading. If you can't tell, the picture I drew in the corner
is of a scorpion in an amulet on a chain I wear under my dress

near my heart. This place was once water, but now
it is sand. There is so much I want to tell you, but
I have not eaten in three days and the fire you built

is just cinders. You once asked me how I could be married
to him, but look who died and look who lived; look who I'm
drawing pictures of scorpions for. I can't feel my legs.

I don't think you'll be back in time. Listen: after
you read this, you will be burned in a terrible accident.
You will forget my name and the shape of the land

you spent your life's work learning, but you will
never forget that you left me to die. My light
is gone. I am writing to you now in the darkness.

In the dark times, will there be singing? Yes. There will be singing about the dark times.

Bertolt Brecht

No matter how disappointed you've been in the past, no matter how weary and resigned you've become, I know that you can now choose a path that will enable you to find and welcome your beloved joyfully. For, truly, there is someone for everyone. Take heart and be not discouraged. Love belongs to all of us.

Katherine Woodward Thomas

SWF ISO tall, dark and handsome
entomologist for Panamanian adventure.

Must not fear Colombian rebel groups,
or refer to ex-girlfriends with fondness.

The latter is non-negotiable. Please
be prepared for foot and mouth disease,

mosquitoes in the jungle after dusk,
no cell phone reception, the consequences

of taking German in high school,
and the world's largest predator bird.

Pic for pic. I am a former debutante
with a trust fund who suffers seizures

accompanied by musical hallucinations.
I hear Mahler's *Kindertotenlieder.* Friends

say I'm a helpless romantic. (You would be, too,
if you lost your entire family to a flash flood.)

I recently returned from a six-month spiritual retreat
and the only thing missing in my life now is danger.

When replying, please indicate whether or not
you own a dugout canoe. I will provide enough

U.S. currency to bribe the insurgency and
on New Year's Eve we will enter the swampland.

CALLING IN THE ONE

The first rule of *Calling in "The One": 7 Weeks*
to Attract the Love of Your Life is don't talk
about calling in the one. The second rule is

surround yourself with people who care for you
enough to tell you that you're better off alone
so that if and when you do find "The One," it's like

the most surprising thing ever. 95% of those
surveyed said they'd been hurt in the past,
but only 94% wanted to talk about it

on a first date. Katherine Woodward Thomas,
M.A., M.F.T., tells us, "Take heart and be not
discouraged." When asked what her heart seeks,

Jennifer (not her real name) said a cold place,
like Siberia, where she would never have to leave
the house at all. This is just one example

of how we set ourselves up to end our lives
alone in remote places where by the time
our bodies are found they are unrecognizable.

After our friends don't want to hear us talk
about this anymore, Katherine Woodward Thomas
invites us to buy diaries where our hearts may speak

freely. She quotes Meggy Wang (not her real name),
who once made perfume out of rose petals
with her brother in their backyard and when

they gave some to their mother, she said,
"Mei you shi ching bu neng jie jue," which
the author was unable to translate, but if you ask

Meggy she will tell you. My diary says things like
"I doubt he could even keep a goldfish alive," and,
"if I was alone on a deserted island and could only bring

one book it would not be yours, Katherine. It would not
be yours." In response to, "Describe a childhood trauma
that you believe is preventing you from finding the one,"

I wrote, "When I was four I wanted to name our kitten
She-Ra and my mom wouldn't let me." And then I felt
uncertain, a little ashamed, so I ripped out the page

and burned it and put the ashes in an envelope and
mailed them to the address of the house I grew up in.
There is an entire chapter devoted to what we remember

of our first house. When Meggy Wang thinks of hers
she thinks of her first girlfriend and stalkers. Aaron
thinks, "Oh my God why did they paint it like that."

Katherine tells us that our feelings about this house
are the same sad feelings we feel about our low
relationship IQ. We leave, new people move in,

and yet we drive by in the middle of the night,
hoping they'll have the blinds open so we can see
inside and feel worse about ourselves. Dear Katherine,

I wrote in my diary today, I asked him if I should
have surgery so my ears don't stick out so far and
he said no, and it was the most romantic thing

anyone has ever said to me. Is he "The One"?
What should I do? Write back soon.
In two weeks we leave the country.

The way you say pianist reminds me of a love story.
You can face the wall until you can make a better face

than that one. Anyway, we went to see the abortion movie
everyone was talking about, and we went to the Pink Pony,

which is really yellow and sans any small gentle horses, and I
ordered a peanut butter and banana sandwich because I was too
     upset

to look at meat and imagine it inside me. He ordered steak.
The February darkness was forgotten outside as we swallowed

in the lamplight, staring at each other's hands, wishing they
     would do
tricks. As I thought about my uterus, he told me about his
     wristwatch.

I love my wristwatch, he said, I love it. You are probably
     thinking
it's inappropriate to roll up your sleeves at the table just to show

you have something to hide and I shouldn't have cried then,
as I stared at the dark hairs below his shirtcuff. I didn't cry.

Let me tell you what I used to do with scissors, I said, and I told
him. And then he waited for someone to come refill our glasses,

I waited for someone to bring a scalpel set. I wanted violence,
someone to fight in the dirty slushed gutters of Ludlow Street.

He was too small to fight, though; I had to wear flats. What are you
thinking? I said. Right now? Nothing. Nothing? Nothing.

I was thinking of being plundered by a Viking. The least
he could have done was put his hands on me in the dark.

You know how cold that winter was. You know what I mean
when I say whaling harpoon. You've seen pictures of what I want.

A BRIEF HISTORY OF MY LIFE PART VII

I can't go to the east village anymore
because it is like going on a tour

of my worst dates. I get older, my heart
leaps at the sight of children

who don't belong to me, I pronounce
everything like an Italian opera title.

I used to listen to songs and have someone
in mind for the you parts, now I just want

to be where the light is intense, I want
the kind of heat that kills you

if you drive into it unprepared. This
isn't a metaphor for anything else.

When I speak of the light, I mean the light.
I go to church and sing along and feel

just as moved as if my faith were blind.
When I speak of the blind, I mean

the light. Truly the only things Lindsey Lohan and I
have in common are our preoccupations

with fame and weight loss, and yet I recognize
a kinship there, as if those two things mattered

more than anything. When I speak of
the darkness, I mean this living.

In a restaurant called Caracas,
I once spent fifteen minutes arguing

about an Ayn Rand book because
every time he said *Anthem* I thought

he meant *We the Living* and I said
what dystopia, what about the woman,

and he said what about the Home
of the Infants and I said what

Home of the Infants? What about
loving a man so much you'll sleep

with another man in order to finance
the first man's tuberculosis treatment?

Welcome to Russia, I said, and we
were looking at each other and then

not. I tried to picture Caracas, tried
to leave him for elsewhere, a fever.

In response to your nice message, yes, no, no, no,
only when I'm drinking, I'd love to, and *Anna Karenina*.

In response to the last question regarding what I like
to do for fun, basically I come home from the factory

and first I make a list on my dry erase board of each
part of my life that makes me want to give up and

then I think, which of these things do I have no
control over, and then I erase the entire list and repeat

positive affirmations in the mirror. Do you have any plans
this Saturday? There is this obscure Ethiopian documentary

I've been wanting to see ever since I read about it
in *Documentarian Quarterly* about a young girl

who is forced to spend two years hiding in an annex
with her father, mother, sister, another couple, their

son, and his cat. She keeps a video diary to chronicle
her hopes and dreams and posts it on YouTube.

Today I felt so alone and surrounded I built a fort
underneath my bed and that's why I'm holding

this flashlight up to my face, you guys. I don't
know how much longer I can take this. We are

down the last of the rice. One entire entry
is thirteen minutes of her erasing all the answers

in her crossword puzzle book and then getting up
and going to the window to trace a heart

with an arrow in the dust. Then she prays in a language
we will never understand, and this is the last time

we see her alive because her diaries lead the police
right to the annex. After they're all captured they're

sent deep into the desert where no flowers bloom,
but it's better, somehow, to realize the fragility

of your life in the desert, where the sky is open,
than in a small dark room and so even though they

kill her loved ones and rob her of her humanity she
kisses the earth. When I am overwhelmed and

double-checking the locks and the windows
and re-organizing the knife drawer again

and washing my hands because I've forgotten
if I've already washed them or not, I think

I hear her voice and she is telling me I'm not
alone. She says it's not your fault until I sleep.

Let us go then, you and I, to where the yellow
sagebrush lights the sand. Let us go and hide

from ghosts. Make me forget my name.
Make me forget the touch of other hands.

I wrote you a love letter, but it was lost in the fire.
Wolves got it. It put stones in its pockets and
went in too deep. It lit a match on a bridge over
the canyon and swan dived like the kind of bird
that eats the dead. I wrote you a love letter, but
it ran out of ammunition. It couldn't kill
the insurgency and so it slept all night
under a veranda choked with hollyhock and
rue and watermelon vines in the country
where the trees are hollow highways
for soldiers to drive through when on leave.
I wrote you a love letter, but it was just
the first six pages of The Book of Luke, ripped
from a Gideon's Bible I stole from the hotel
I stayed in last week when I was trying
to decide whether or not to steal the Bible.
I read it four times. I found the story I heard
at a wedding once, of the woman who asked
her husband why he never brought home flowers,
like the husband of her friend across the street did,
and her husband told her he hardly knew the woman,
why would he bring her flowers; except in the Bible
it's not a woman, it's a lamb, and it isn't flowers,
it's blood. I wrote you a love letter, but when I went

to that wedding I accidentally left it in the guestbook
instead of my name. Maybe I can get it back, but
if I don't try then I never have to see them again.
In the Book of Lamentations, after the temple
is destroyed, Banksy sits with Jeremiah inside
a cavern near the Damascus gate and says,
As soon as you meet someone you know
the reason you will leave them, and Jeremiah
writes this down so he can get it tattooed later.
What I wouldn't give sometimes for a pen
and a piece of papyrus and a view of the sea
in an apartment paid for by someone else's hard,
manual labor. I wrote you a love letter, but
I will never leave you so you will never need
to find it at the bottom of a drawer only to throw
it away. Have you ever held a fish in your hands
and watched the breath go in and out like horses,
thinking, I'll let you go when I can think of a metaphor
to describe the broken light of all these stars?

R_B_T L_VE S_NG

Today I think I said why are you trying to hurt me
at least four times to a large crowd of people and
then I came home and ate vanilla frozen yogurt

and listened to my mom tell me all about
optimal heart rhythms and the application
that is supposed to help us do this, optimize

our hearts, so that we will have a higher tolerance
for emotional pain, like robots do. If a robot is sad
a robot will make cookies shaped like velociraptors

and leave work early just to mail some to his
mom. If a robot is really sad he will draw hearts
and arrows and blood on every smooth surface.

If a robot is totally devastated he will go on an online dating
site and under "Who I'm looking for" write, "Someone
to teach me how to love." Then the robot will stare

at this, wonder if it makes him seem like he just wants
sex, and write, "Someone to hurt me. I am a robot."
He will list his interests as parasailing, infinite regressions,

and vegetarianism, and then go change the water
in his guinea pig cage while he waits for the three thousand
eligible women to come break down the door to the house

he lives in with his mom and his guinea pig, Rumi.
Sometimes when a robot feels really sad he will
post fake emails from people who don't exist on his blog

just to prove to all the people who don't read his blog
that he has friends. Dear Luke, Thank you so much
for last night. It's still hard to walk. Dear Luke, I loved

that poem you posted about staring into the hot,
white sun. Dear Luke, I have two tickets to *Faust*
tonight. Are you free? Love, Me. After three minutes

of staring into the deep abyss of his inbox, Luke
will update his online profile to say he's looking
for a relationship with a girl who signs all of the notes

she gives him "me" with a row of xo. He will change
his interests to pandas, emus, and tae kwon do. He will
post a picture of himself standing in front of a great chasm,

wearing sunglasses with blue tinted lenses. Luke will lie
about his height and religion and what he thinks is sexy.
Hi ladies, my name is Luke. I am a robot. I have leukemia.

RE: HI

Congratulations on Alaska, it sounds really great.
I spoke with your wife yesterday—she didn't know

what to get you since you seem to have everything:
dried figs, firewood, sugar cookie scented candles,

and I said maybe you would like a picture of someone
who loved you, but who wasn't with you in the cave. Like

a woman?, she said. I don't know, I said. You know
him better than I do. I told her I bought you a book

of stories about a Thai man and his adventures
in cockfighting and love, which I hope you've received

because otherwise I just ruined it. I meant to ask you,
though, do you ever see things, out there in the wild,

and wish there was someone standing next to you
so you could point and say, Look? Such as bats?

Or strange lights? Do your dreams take place
in different weather? So many things happened

this year that I just didn't have the courage to write
them down on paper and then photocopy it and then

mail it to people I don't talk to anymore just to show
I'm still alive, but I hope you at least sent something

that says you're in Alaska now. There might be
those who miss you and would want to know

where you are so they can pray in your direction.
Not that you need it. You were always so solitary

and reckless in the good sense. I found a picture
of us from when we were children, our eyes

alight with matching blue-green expectancy, our teeth
missing in the same spots, our arms outstretched,

holding the pigeons we had caught in our hands.
Do you remember at what point you let yours go?

IMMORTALITY

At the gym, they told me I would not die,
I would only get sexier, and I believed them.

I spent my nights wondering if this was going to turn
into something long-term, if this was what is meant by casual,

or if this was just my annual catastrophic disappointment
because if it wasn't, then I would have to brace

myself. I took my medication and looked at pictures
of people who were not in love with me. I deleted

their names from my cache, said hello to my cat
over the phone, took more medication. Days

passed. I learned it's hard to measure your own increasing
sexiness. I enlisted bystanders. I passed mirrors

and pretended they were not mirrors, but clean
windows, and I was not myself, I was

a clean stranger. Some days I was sure
she wanted to come home with me, and

I had to let her down easy, through the window,
like a priest. Once I'd been unleashed

from thoughts of my own death I was free
to be loved in the way I always knew I'd deserved:

reciprocally, in Fiji, our bodies lithe and bronzed
like gods, but at the same time I felt like a vampire,

and none of my friends could relate. They were jealous
of my book deal, my time spent at the ashram

while they were here, suffering another winter,
their unsexiness a fluorescent sign that blinks all night.

A BRIEF HISTORY OF MY LIFE PART XXVI

I can't go to the east village anymore
because that's where all the ghosts are.

Yes, I went and got older again.
I made the mistake of having a birthday

and taking it to the mansion
where birthdays fall down stairs

and break their necks. Be careful.
I've never been comfortable before

and you should know that.
You should know I've outlived

everyone in my family, and now
I'm your guide to the haunted

universe. Watch out for pianos.
Take my picture if you want

to see what color my energy is.
In the dark I'm either pretty or sad-

colored, and my silhouette might exceed
your expectations. Out with the old,

in with the nude, as they say.
Say you want a ghost to stay.

Say you light some candles. Say
you lure her with sadness because

ghosts are hungry for palpitations.
Say you try to hold her but you're never sure

if it's tight enough. We're the ghosts
and we're here to tell you:

it's never tight enough. You'll never
keep us from floating up

and down the staircase like memories
you didn't even know you'd lost.

No one wants to watch me break
my neck, so watch me disappear.

I can't go to the east village anymore
because I'm already here in the dark.

HAVE YOU HUGGED A LATVIAN TODAY?

Miss Nicaragua was born in a village you've never
even heard of, and she reads Michael Crichton

paperbacks aloud to impoverished young women
to improve their English so that they, too,

may some day enter the Miss Universe Pageant.
I couldn't find any socks that matched this morning.

Miss Japan is 5'8". Miss Japan loves horses. She
says she wants to be a spokeswoman for pediatric

AIDS, or toxic shock syndrome, or aphasia
or something, but it gets lost in translation, and

I'm like, I wish, right? I wish there was
a spokeswoman for aphasia who

was also internationally recognized for her
beauty, intellect, and equestrian panache.

During the commercial break, my boyfriend
tells me about this girl who makes the best

mix tapes "ever," and I'm like, What's her name?
What does she look like? But all he'll say

is that I'm sitting too close to him on the couch again.
Not even her eye color or anything. Then he starts

to ask how much an MRI is because he believes
he has all the symptoms indicative of a brain

tumor, but when the show comes back on
I'm like, Shh. Watch. Do you think Miss Nairobi

had her teeth done? Do you think Miss Slovenia
comes from a broken home? My parents

put me in ballet when I was a child, but still—
I'm nervous about moving to Albuquerque

so I practice by sitting on the balcony
of our apartment in the sun and reading

The Unbearable Lightness of Being while
keeping in mind the humidity factor, and

how, in the desert, it will be a *dry* heat. Everybody
says that. Everybody specifies. Even Miss Mexico

would if you asked her. I had hoped Miss
United Arab Emirates would make it

to the top five, but of course they gave it
to Miss Nepal. The judges are: Michelle Kwan,

David Hasselhoff, and the ghost of Virginia Woolf.
Once again, I wish. As Miss South Africa put it,

It wasn't nails that held Jesus to the cross. It
was love. And you know what? I am going to .

make my boyfriend the best mix tape ever *ever*.
It will have a song by Joy Division, followed

by "How Deep Is the Ocean," followed
by an acoustic cover of "Hey Ya,"

followed by a Bach cello suite, and I
will call the mix, "Let's Leave the State

Together." Should we tell our parents?
What would Miss Korea do? Now she's

walking, floating, across the stage, like
it's the length of a desert in a country

she's never seen, and when she makes
it to the end they ask her what she sees

in her future, but we never get to hear
her answer because the moment she

starts to speak the heel of her shoe breaks off
and she falls into her translator's arms.

A good girlfriend never cries and when she sits
it's in the splits because she's a gymnast, or
used to be, or wants to be, or something, and
this is why you love her. Because she's a go-getter.
Because she picks you up in her Chevy Silverado
and she keeps her tandem bicycle in the back, and
a blanket, and she knows the shortcut to the ravine.
In my town there are no ravines. In my town they named
the street that runs through the viaduct under the train tracks
Covered Bridge Road, and I believe this to be intentionally
misleading. One time I told this to a friend, but all she said
was, Is that the end of the story? Was that even a story?
It wasn't the end, but I didn't like her tone so I said yes,
all sarcastic, and then I stopped returning her phone calls.
A good girlfriend waits up for you when you're out
starting fires. A good girlfriend would help you steal
a car. In other words, if it means buying a blonde wig
and a fake I.D. and never going back to Sioux Falls,
never looking back over her shoulder at what could
or might have been for fear she'll turn to a pillar of salt,
even if it means living in sin in Tijuana, okay, yes,
sure, I will help you steal that car. Because I remember
when you asked me to help you love me, and I think
this is what you meant. For nineteen years we were like
two ants from different hills whose paths would never cross

because it was not predestined in the stars, but now
you ask how long I'd wait if you were in prison and
I hold out my arms to indicate that I love you
as much as polar bears love ice floes because there aren't
enough anymore and the polar bears are drowning.
I didn't even know what a chlorofluorocarbon was
until I met you. When I was a young girl
in Sunday school at the Universalist Church
we often made Native American drums
to pound the rhythms of our hearts' secret desires,
but sometimes we made macaroni jewelry, and
in the spring the cicadas came we got snow shovels
and cleared the shells from the sidewalks under
the old elms, singing, Let beauty, truth, and good
be sung, through every land, by every tongue.
I remember Tyler found a live one and plucked
its wings and was reprimanded by the same woman
who told me when I asked what I should believe in that
I could believe in "anything." I found out later that what
she meant was that universalism means God loves me
so much that he wouldn't create me if He thought
I was unsalvageable, but at the time I thought, okay,
of course I believe in Beatrix Potter and Millard Fillmore
and trees, but what if I grow up and decide that insects
have no souls; what if I grow up to be the kind of girl
who throws away the drums she made and disregards
the law and finds herself in the backseats of cars

with someone's hand in her hair and she likes it
so much she decides to become a girl who asks
for such a thing. What congregation would open their arms
and their hearts to her? Where could she go to learn the songs
she'd have to know before she could even go to where
the congregation who was going to open their arms to her
met each week? And which of these stories will I tell my
    children?
Will I tell them to believe in anything or will I specify,
will I buy them butterfly nets, will I buy them rackets,
will I dream at night that they're taken from me,
will I teach them to swim or hire someone or drop them
in the water and see if they drown? Maybe they'll walk.
Maybe I'll have no children. Maybe I'll miscarry and
take up oil painting and brew iced tea in the sun while you
are out collecting cattle skulls and when you come home
to me we'll stare at the map on the wall and throw darts.

IV

The distinction between past, present, and future
is only a stubbornly persistent illusion.

Albert Einstein

DISPATCH FROM THE FUTURE

In the future, I'm your mother.
My name is Carol.

I hold you when you want me
to and I don't ask

questions.

I never call your name
when I lose sight of you

in public.

In the future, we're discreet.

We live forever

or seem to.

We upholster our lives with secrets
and our holsters are concealable.

When you want me
to, I hold you

like a wife
in Valparaiso.

You say, *Tell me something
else*, and I do

all sorts of tricks.

DISPATCH FROM THE FUTURE

In the future, we are all about safety
and its sister, schadenfreude.

We stay in our houses
and sell our selves on the Internet.

We no longer refer to it as the apocalypse.

In the future, those who can afford to feed themselves
on sun. We eat with our shoulders. We run

towards the past, where we buried our fear,
just in case we missed it in the future.

I miss ignorance. I miss caring less.
I miss hope's stubborn blindness.

Every single man I've ever loved is walking down the aisle
on Sunday. Which aisle is mine? And where is my husband?

Maybe a dingo ate my husband.

What I left I left unfinished.
Take care of yourself, it all said;

we'll be fine, we'll finish

in your absence, but fish
cannot find their way out

of water: that's the hitch

of this illness. My hypnotist
suggested a horse

for fastest departure.

I said ship. At the end
of the day it's your odyssey,

she said, and then brought me back

to wakefulness, this room,
this view of the sea, a little ship

tethered at the fence like a willing

animal, and I thought yes, this
wishful thinking works:

I'll be a believer and leave.

REVISIONISM

Going to the airport, opalescent sky,
dawn dragging its feet through the river, I'm

thinking that anyone who says I'll make it up to you

is a person aimed for future let-downs,
is a person who forgets anniversaries, but

I've forgiven worse. I've driven to Amarillo

in one day and one night, through St. Louis
and Cuba, Missouri, where an old Coke facade

hung like a stage prop above the gas station,

through Miami, Oklahoma, where there were birds
and cottonwoods and Do Not Drive Through Smoke

signs and we wondered what could be burning

along a highway with so few exits, but by then
we were half-asleep and so when I say birds

I am inventing them. I am a revisionist.

I am giving my life back to myself, only
better, brighter, faster. Everything happens

at dawn for a reason. At night I find myself

reaching for a light switch that isn't there.
Or reaching for a song. Reaching for a shovel

so I can go back and plant magnolias

along I-44, give the girl in the passenger seat
a silk scarf for her hair, and unleash doves

above the road like wedding rice,

like a flag of surrender. This version
of events is just as true as any other.

Ask me when I'm older. Ask what I remember.

TRAVEL BROCHURE FOR THE FUTURE

We have this lush AstroTurf here.
We have these incredible windows.

Forget what's left to do at home.

We have sky.

We have what you miss about the past and
we have masks so you can dress up

like the person you wish you were. Name two

things you'd rather do than be here
with me, now, in the hinterland.

When the river floods, we'll swim

to safety.

When the river floods, we'll start

an ancient civilization.

Let's call it Egypt.

Everything anyone has ever loved
about you has come from the future

in the form of a vision, a wish, or a sympathy;

that's why they say I knew you would
do that, I knew we would end up

like this.

DISPATCH FROM THE FUTURE

I am wearing my librarian costume.
Yes, I saved it from the fires.

In the future, when we say antiquity, we mean
state fairs and musicals. We mean affairs

of state, amusement. You left me a message
to say you were sad but you understood
which state I was coming from and I'm wondering

now which state you meant. West of us?
Or did you mean a state of mind?

I don't have states of mind, I only have sweater sets.

I get dressed up and then I undress. I'd show you,
but this is a dispatch. I'm the dispatcher.

The calls come into my call center and
it's my job to say, What's the future

of your emergency?

Our new state flag is an aurochs—
not to celebrate extinction, but

to celebrate the wild part of us that died
in 1627. They moved her skull to Stockholm.

I wear my state flag like a dress.

DISPATCH FROM THE FUTURE

In the future, you live in Switzerland
and you come to see us sometimes

but I wish you could see us now.

We're certainly missable.

We're certainly sexy

in a way that only gets better
with age. As a child,

I was not even a little bit sexy.

I lived at a boarding school
and I owned only one sweater,

two cassette tapes, three pieces
of string, and all my organs.

Were they keeping us alive
for our poetry?

Of course not.

They were keeping us alive
for our lungs.

They were keeping our mothers
from us.

The closer I get to completion,
the closer I want to hold you

in the make believe moonlight.

PLEASE HANDLE YOUR CHILDREN

When I see my one particular enemy I am filled with laughter
and the good times, as if I do not know he sees through me

as, how do you say, the fog? Do you know this reconciliation,
as moderated by the United Nations? I thought we could

send our representatives in the form of poets.
My poet would have this letter to say, All the leaves

have trees. His poet would have this letter to say,
My client no longer wishes to see your client except

as the fog. I am that child behind you on this airplane.
I am screaming to hear the sound of my voice.

Someone put me on regular sleep schedule please.
Someone else tell my enemy I know he sees me.

Then forget representatives. Let us send ghosts
to act out our, how do you say, erotic dance?

I know I am a child because I have been
to more bar mitzvahs than funerals.

I know I am a child because in the fields
of ocean out the airplane window, I see

fear. Do you want to be knowing
if this is based on true story?

When I see my one particular enemy
I want to lie down and, how do you say,

give it up. I am his enemy but he is not
mine. I am a child. Please to handle me.

REVISIONISM

Listening to you in your sleep, pretending
this is just as good as if I were asleep myself,

the tender evening behind us like a jet trail

that wants to be read as a cloud and it looks
like a tiger tonight. I'm pretending your arms

are your arms, which is to say I'm not

pretending they belong to someone else,
good for me, but I'm still not above keeping track

of the anniversaries of everything I'm brokenhearted

over and this goes for men, departures
and arrivals, weddings I was not invited to

for good reason, achievements of my enemies.

I'm thinking of rewriting history so instead of jealousy
my major themes are revenge and justice, and

I'm going to the airport so we can miss each other more,

because I want a future to look forward to,
another new year already, noisemakers

and dry champagne and songs I know

the words to and the way you looked at me
at the costume party: I want another chance

for second chances. I never make the same mistake

more than four or twelve times, but enough
about you, tell me more about you.

Someone told me that my life would be easy
because my face looks like this.

Did I win any prizes this week? No.

And guess what else? I don't belong to you.

I hate to be the one

to tell you, but phones are no longer in use.
Please be patient while we try and fix this.

We thank you for your patience.

We're putting your patience on our daily
gratitude list. We're getting our harmonicas

and we're standing in a row
in our farmer's wife dresses.

Dispatch from the future:

I have all the time in the world
and I don't want to spend any of it.

Dispatch from the future:

when I say I want to take off all my clothes
I don't mean what if we had sex. I mean listen

to the sublime: sun on my shoulders, God in my ear.

Dispatch from the future:

life is only too short if you are having a good time.

ADDENDUM TO THE PREVIOUS DISPATCH

I just remembered every single thing I've ever done
and now I'm embarrassed. I want my afterlife

guaranteed, so I have ordered a tomb built at Giza

for my remains. They are as follows: all my clothes,
my harmonica, my body, letters to my enemies.

The dictionary says you can refer to everyone

who will be alive in the future as prosperity so
Dear Prosperity, I used to live in the future,

too, but I fear the past is a brushfire

and I am a prairie. Now that I have what I asked for
I see I should have been more specific.

True: time travel is tricky, but backwards
is easier than forwards because at least you know

the way. In my memory it is always autumnal
and my weight approximately seven stones. Birds

fly in droves, dervishes to their bird god
on their way to Florida, and in their memories

it seems always a season for leaving. I watch them
hover above the temple where the police

officer stands guard each Sabbath. I watch them
while I listen to someone tell me about weddings

where he comes from, how the groom must choose
his bride blindfolded, from among her friends and

sisters, feeling their bodies one by one down the line,
checking for familiars. When I say choose I mean

remember. When I say remember I can't forget
Konstantin, how he asked to carry my purse

through the arboretum in July and let me know
his mother is widowed in Kiev, though his father

is still alive. As far as he knows. As far as he can throw
a stone. When I time travel, I go to Oregon and skip

stones with the boyfriend I left for a map, the sister
who may one day stand in line at my wedding

to be caressed by the blind. True: when the seasons
change, I get like this. It is a little like gymnastics

and a little like a pelvic examination:
uncomfortable, routine, and sometimes

my life is at stake. I used to have a friend
who got like this too, someone to go to yoga

with at the end of the world, but then
she found god and alternative methods

of contraception and now we speak
in halting cadence, like women

from different tribes, separated
by a river, a river filled with stones,

a river you could only get to if you
were from Kansas and thought you could fly

around the waistline of the world,
until you crashed somewhere

in the Pacific, never to be found.
I feel autumnal tonight. Let's go

to the future, where our bird god
lives, and ask for stronger wings.

WANT AD FROM THE FUTURE

I just realized I am out of currency, food, and time.
I am, how do you say, bereft of necessity.

Not only you were at that party, but your wife
was dressed like a board game and she spoke

to me of every thing that matters not at all.
Want ad from the future: we are seeking

anonymity. Birds came. They told me
I would be more happier without a face.

I said but what about these enemies.
The birds said even with no face

your enemies will know you
by your body. I said let us

get rid of it then. I am,
how do you say, not having

a body anymore. Hello
from the future, where

we are seeking reasons
to keep our clothes on.

Except me. I have no shoulders.
I fed them to this dingo.

I'VE WRITTEN ALL OVER THIS IN HOPES YOU CAN READ IT

Welcome to sparkly tomorrowland.
We have prepared this room for your arrival.

We hope you like the view.
We hope you like the Nile.

Birds came; they told us a mournful
cadence and a flustered two-step

is your kind of Friday night and
we said we'd never seen

this kind of trembling before.

Blame the colonizers, the birds
said, before flying off to Oaxaca,

never to be seen again. Yes,
there are people here, but only if you

want there to be people

here. We can cater. Our people
are puppets and our puppets

are incredibly lifelike, like people.

Most of our staff will not bother you,
but anyone who does we guarantee

will be hot, and covered in spring grasses.

No regrets. And no hope either.

We pride ourselves on this:

somewhere, it is already tomorrow.

DISPATCH FROM THE FUTURE

In the future, we pay our debts with blood.
Always more where that came from.

And the white noise sounds like sun.
Lily, I'm gonna run

and run

until I'm back where I started.
I'm gonna invert my body, bathe

my brain in blood.

This is a devotional.
Lily, don't cry.
This is a devotional.
Listen to the sun.

Isn't there some Eden we can meet in?
Bring your prayer

to your third eye.

In the future, we temper our irreverence
with beauty. What a stunner, we tell

our ancestors, retroactively.

I used to have to try so hard to look
like I wasn't trying and now look:

I'm bending to the altar wall.

This is a devotional for the living.

Lily, don't fear the future.
I'm in it. We're here.

DISPATCH FROM THE FUTURE

In the future, we are tender.

We temper our irreverence
with intimacy.

It's, like, slightly wonderful.

We pronounce magic
like we're from Michigan,
and all our mothers continue
mothering, like harbors,

indefinitely.

There's a sense of indeterminacy
with mothering and we take

turns standing like breakwaters.

Life is dangerous, wild, and yet
we welcome it.

We're in therapy.
It's called water.

DISPATCH FROM THE FUTURE

Yes, I am writing to you from there.
Yes, in the future, we have excitement.

Also: a forgiveness economy.

All IOUs are tied to balloon
strings and released into the atmosphere
in an environmentally responsible way.

Lunch is free for everybody. Lunch
is peanut butter sandwiches, sliced
on the diagonal, by mothers. We are sparkly.

Everything is pleasure, but we are
also acutely empathetic, like children.

When one starts crying, another answers.

A fugue state.

We are sparkly but we also remember
what it was like before we were. We can
relate to our past selves: dull like mercury,

alluvial soil, just after the earthquake.
It's hard to know which disaster to expect, yet

no one ever thinks, I don't want to do anything
except sleep forever maybe. Yes, in the future

we are prepared for what we cannot prepare
for. We are sparkly for a reason, our country

depends on us for a kind of warning entertainment.

In the future we never make pilgrimages to disaster
sites, we lay flowers on the brows of the living.

ACKNOWLEDGEMENTS

Thank you to the editors of the following journals, in which some of these poems first appeared: *Absent, Bat City Review, Can We Have Our Ball Back?, Catch Up, Diagram, h-ngm-n, horseless review, InDigest Magazine, Jellyroll, LIT, Low Rent, MiPOesias, No Tell Motel, Nöo Journal, Ocho, OH NO, Sixth Finch, Softblow,* and *Washington Square.*

Many poems also appeared in these chapbooks: *How to Mend a Broken Heart with Vengeance* (Dancing Girl Press), *Summer in Paris* (Mondo Bummer), and *The Future Comes to Those who Wait* (Grey Book Press).

The poem that begins "In the future, you live in Switzerland," takes much of its content from a letter Elizabeth Hildreth's five-year-old daughter wrote to their Swiss foreign exchange student, Julia.

The poem that begins "In the future, we pay our debts with blood," is dedicated with love to Lily Ladewig.

The title "I've Written All Over This in Hopes You Can Read It" came to me in an email from Nate Pritts.

"Epistolaphobia" is a word Edna St. Vincent Millay invented to describe the feeling of being unable to write letters.